play guitar with...
eric clapton

usic Sales' complete catalogue describes thousands
titles and is available in full colour sections by subject,
rect from Music Sales Limited.
ease state your areas of interest and send a
eque/postal order for £1.50 for postage to:
usic Sales Limited, Newmarket Road,
ry St. Edmunds, Suffolk IP33 3YB.

Exclusive Distributors:
Music Sales Limited
8-9 Frith Street,
London W1V 5TZ, England.
Music Sales Pty Limited
120 Rothschild Avenue,
Rosebery, NSW 2018, Australia.

Order No. AM950862
ISBN 0-7119-3312-X
This book © Copyright 1997
by Wise Publications

Compiled by Peter Evans
Music arranged by Arthur Dick
Music processed by The Pitts
Cover design by Pearce Marchbank
Computer layout by Ben May
Photographs courtesy of
London Features International

Printed in the United Kingdom by
Caligraving Limited, Thetford, Norfolk.

Wise Publications
London/New York/Paris/Sydney/Copenhagen/Madrid

tablature & instructions explained

The tablature stave comprises six lines, each representing a string on the guitar as illustrated.

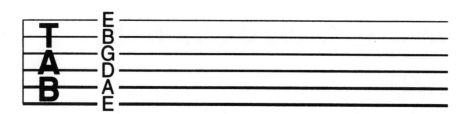

A number on any of the lines indicates, therefore, the string and fret on which a note should be played.

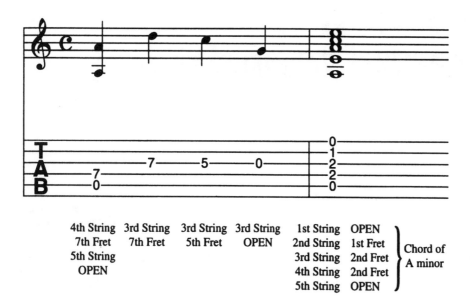

4th String	3rd String	3rd String	3rd String	1st String	OPEN	
7th Fret	7th Fret	5th Fret	OPEN	2nd String	1st Fret	Chord of
5th String				3rd String	2nd Fret	A minor
OPEN				4th String	2nd Fret	
				5th String	OPEN	

A useful hint to help you read tablature is to cut out small squares of self-adhesive paper and stick them on the upper edge of the guitar neck adjacent to each of the frets, numbering them accordingly. Be careful to use paper that will not damage the finish on your guitar.

Finger Vibrato

Tremolo Arm Vibrato

Glissando

Strike the note, then slide the finger up or down the fretboard as indicated.

Tremolo Strumming

This sign indicates fast up and down stroke strumming.

8va

This sign indicates that the notes are to be played an octave higher than written.

loco

This instruction cancels the above.

This note-head indicates the string is to be totally muted to produce a percussive effect.

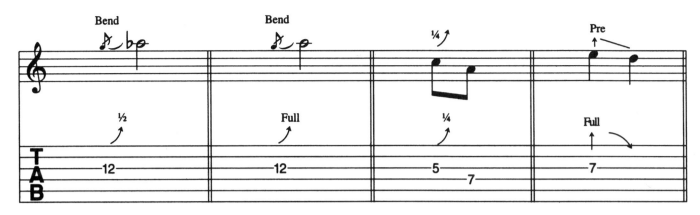

HALF TONE BEND

Play the note G then bend the string so that the pitch rises by a half tone (semi-tone).

FULL TONE BEND

DECORATIVE BEND

PRE-BEND

Bend the string as indicated, strike the string and release.

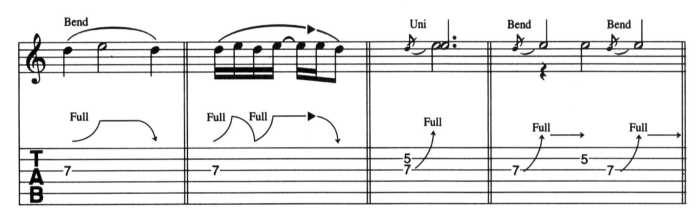

BEND & RELEASE

Strike the string, bend it as indicated, then release the bend whilst it is still sounding.

BEND & RESTRIKE

Strike the string, bend or gliss as indicated, then restrike the string where the symbol occurs.

UNISON BEND

Strike both strings simultaneously then immediately bend the lower string as indicated.

STAGGERED UNISON BEND

Strike the lower string and bend as indicated; whilst it is still sounding strike the higher string.

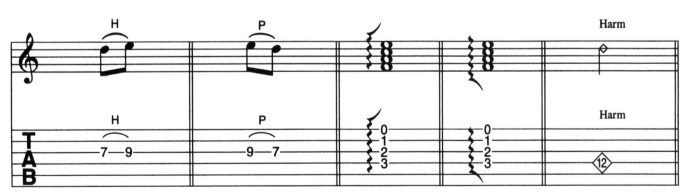

HAMMER-ON

Hammer a finger down on the next note without striking the string again.

PULL-OFF

Pull your finger off the string with a plucking motion to sound the next note without striking the string again.

RAKE-UP   RAKE-DOWN

Strum the notes upwards or downwards in the manner of an arpeggio.

HARMONICS

Strike the string whilst touching it lightly at the fret position shown. Artificial Harmonics, (A.H.), will be described in context.

bad love

Words & Music by Eric Clapton & Mick Jones

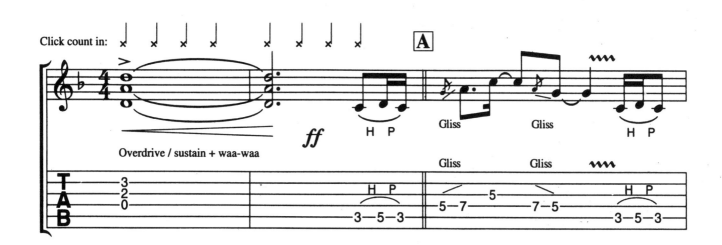

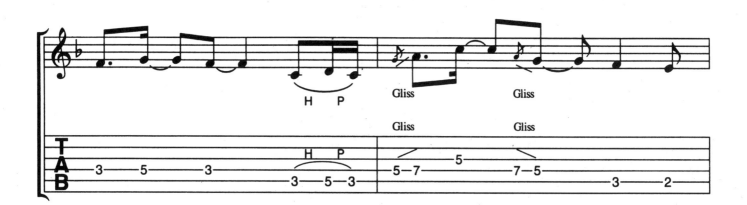

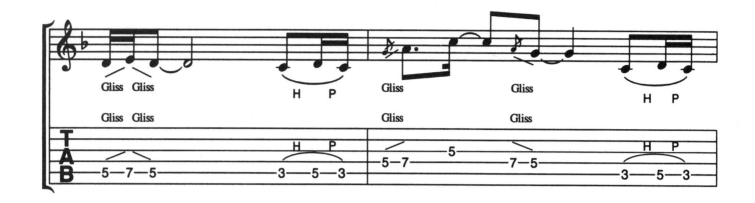

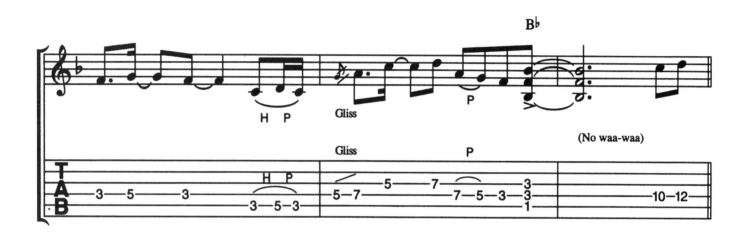

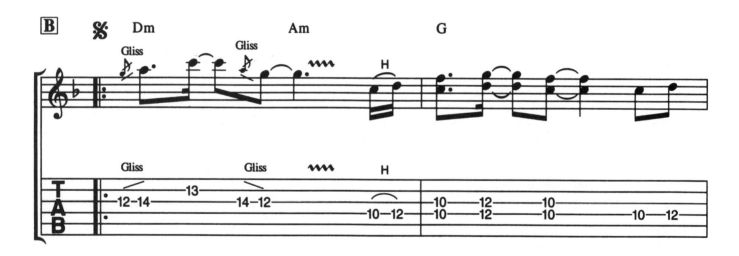

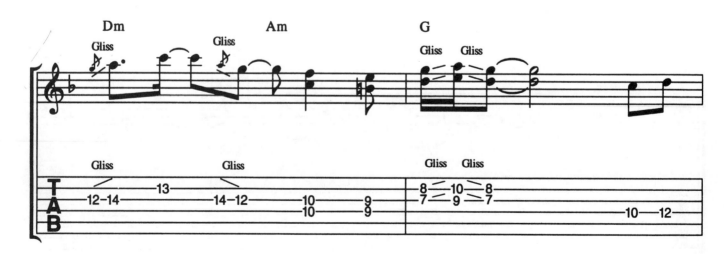

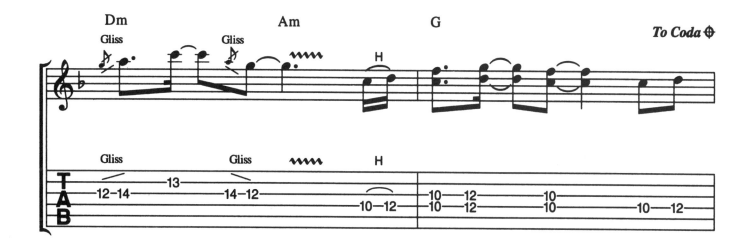

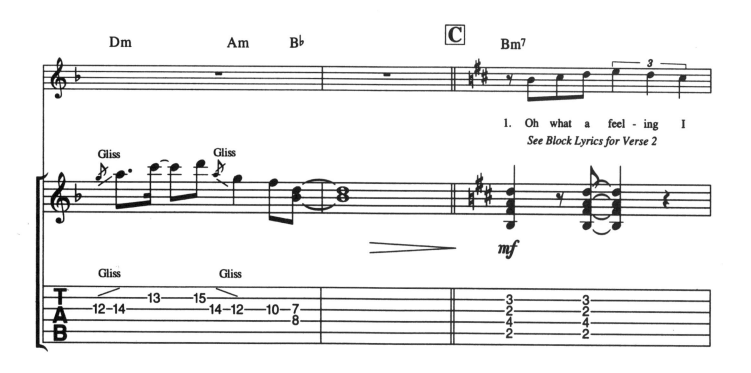

1. Oh what a feel-ing I
See Block Lyrics for Verse 2

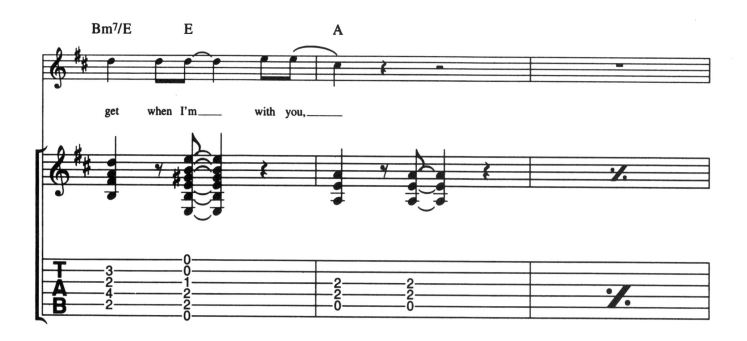

get when I'm___ with you,___

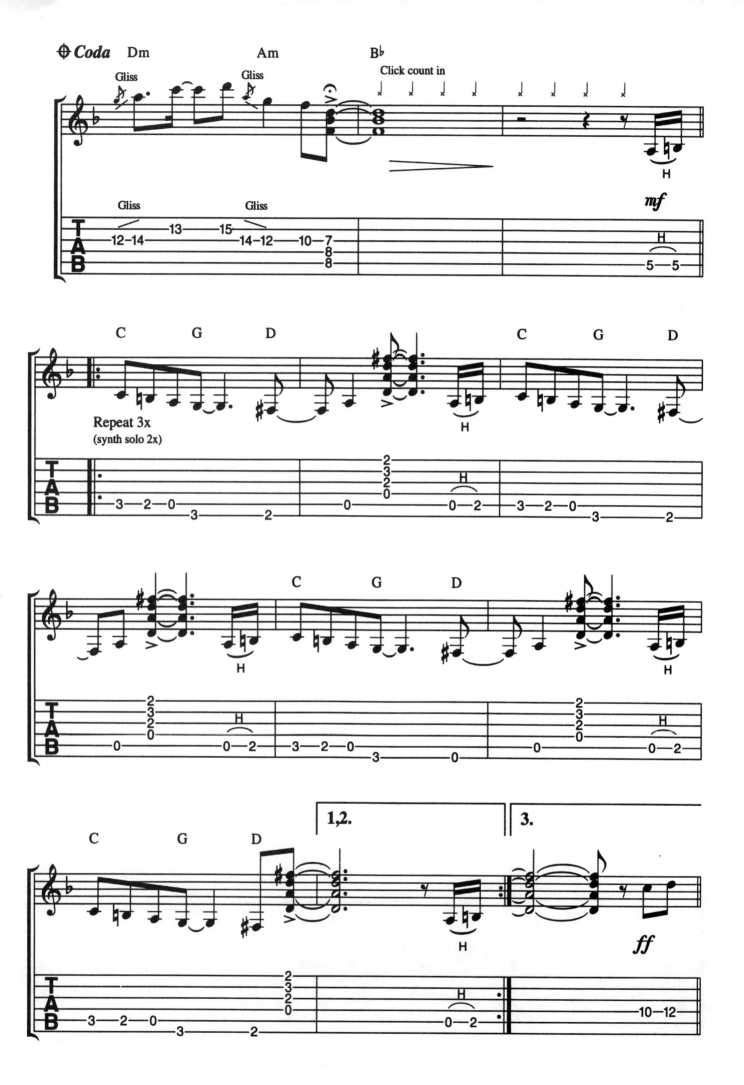

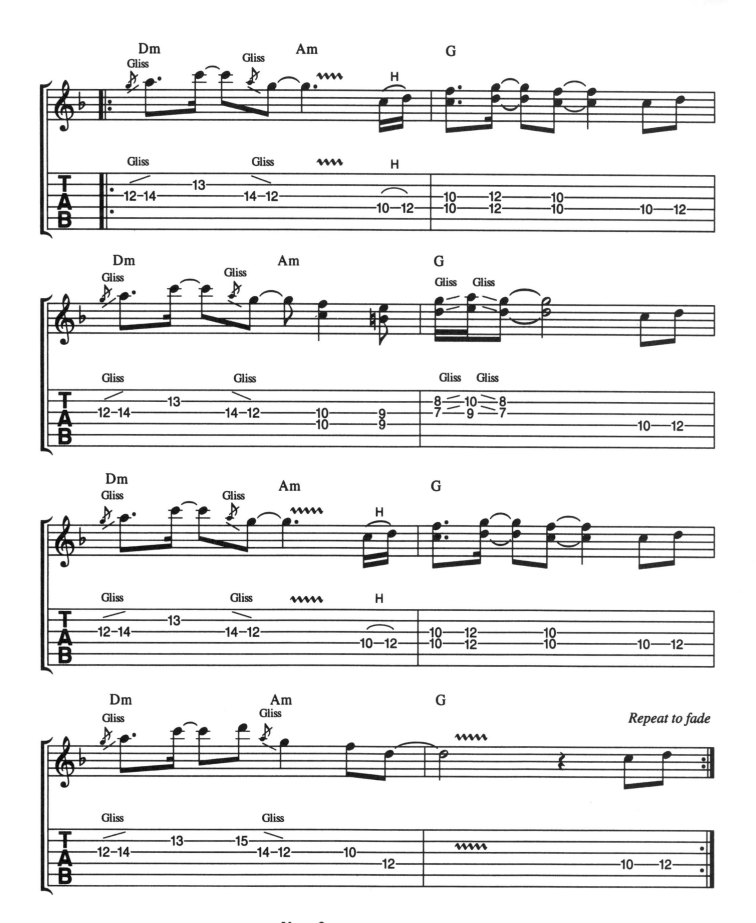

Verse 2:
And now I see that my life has been so cruel
With all the heartaches I had 'til I met you
But I'm glad to say now that's all behind me
With you here by my side
And there's no more memories to remind me
Your love will keep me alive.

i shot the sheriff

Words & Music by Bob Marley

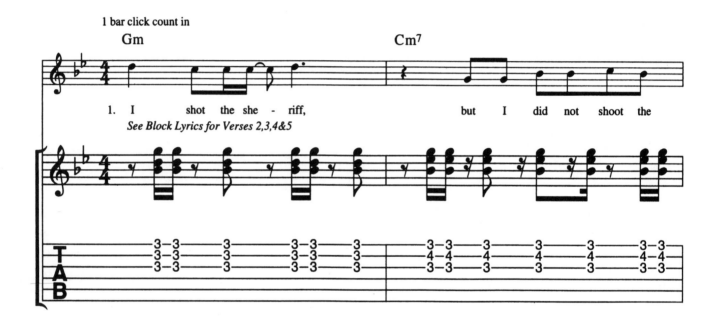

1 bar click count in

1. I shot the she - riff, but I did not shoot the

See Block Lyrics for Verses 2,3,4&5

de - pu - ty. I shot the she - riff,

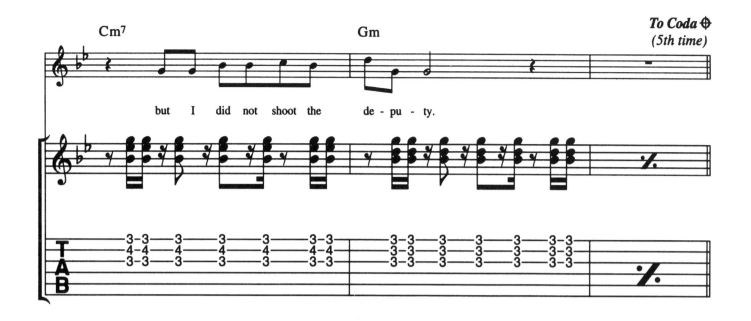

but I did not shoot the de - pu - ty.

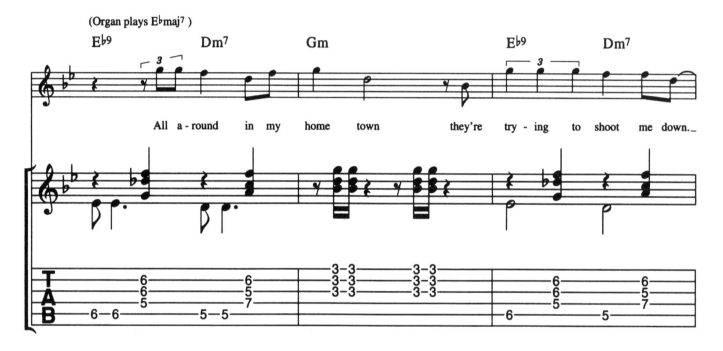

(Organ plays E♭maj7)

All a - round in my home town   they're try - ing to shoot me down.

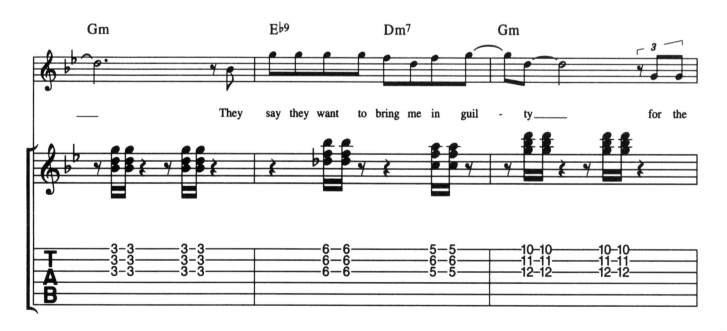

___   They   say they want to bring me in guil - ty___   for the

13

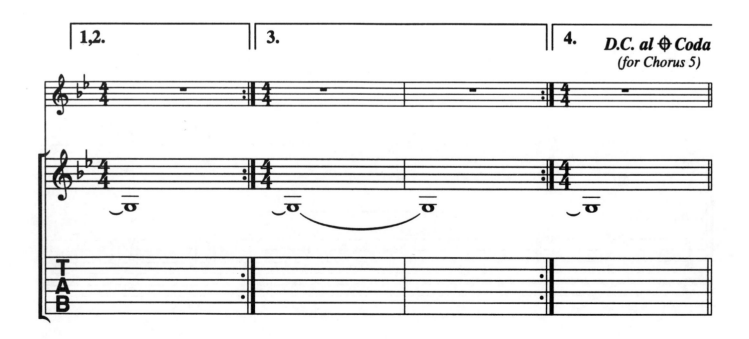

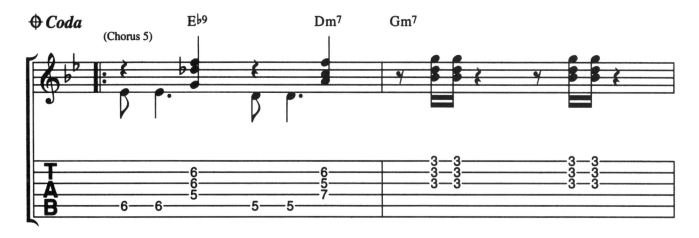

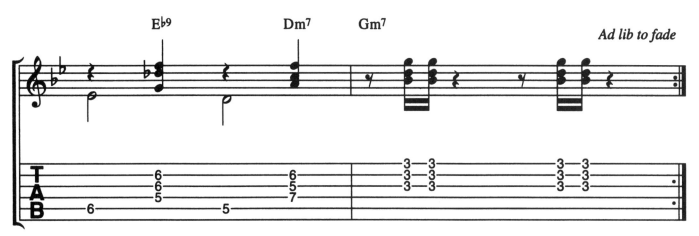

Ad lib to fade

Chorus 2:
I shot the sheriff
But I swear it was in self defence.
I shot the sheriff
And they say it is a capital offence.

Verse 2:
Sheriff John Brown always hated me
For what I don't know
And every time that I plant a seed
He said "Kill it, before it grows"
He said "Kill it, before it grows."

Chorus 3:
I shot the sheriff
But I swear it was in self defence.
I shot the sheriff
And they say it is a capital offence.

Verse 3:
Freedom came my way one day
And I started out of town there.
All of a sudden I see Sheriff John Brown
Aiming to shoot me down
So I shot, I shot him down
And I say, hey.

Chorus 4&5:
I shot the sheriff
But I did not shoot the deputy.
I shot the sheriff
But I did not shoot the deputy.

Verse 4:
Reflexes got the better of me
And what must be, must be.
Every day the bucket goes to the well
But one day the bottom will drop out
Yes, one day the bottom will drop out
But I say,

15

layla

Words & Music by Eric Clapton & Jim Gordon

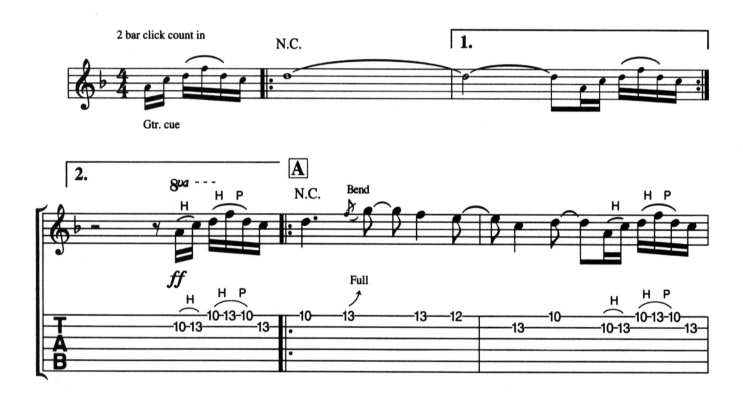

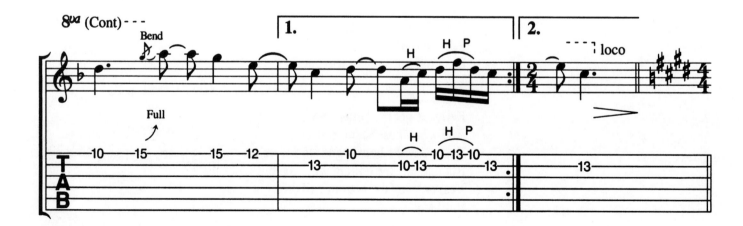

1. What will you do when you get lone - ly?
See Block Lyrics for Verses 2&3
No - bo - dy's wait - ing by your

side.

You've been run - ning and hid - ing much too long,

you know it's just your fool - ish pride. Lay -

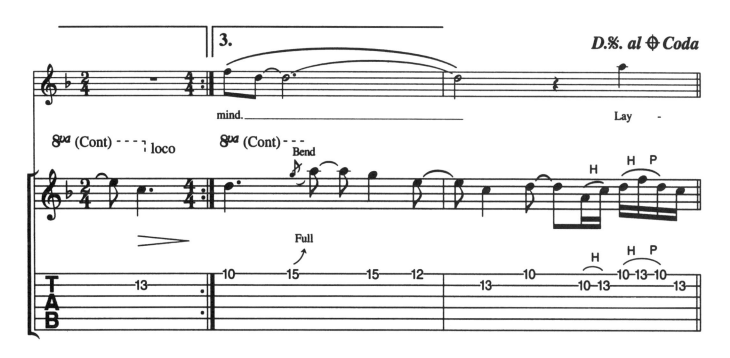

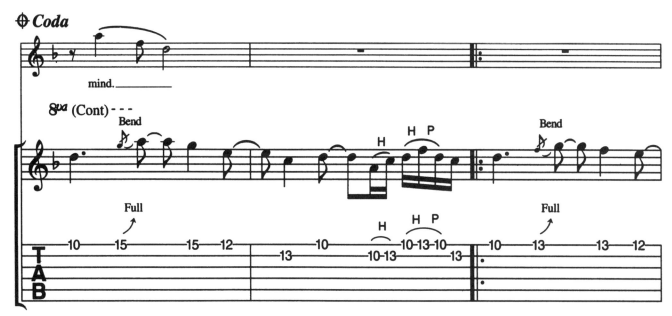

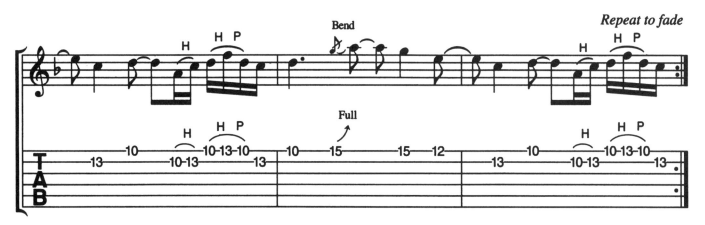

Verse 2:	Verse 3:
Tried to give you consolation	Let's make the best of the situation
Your old man won't let you down.	Before I finally go insane.
Like a fool I fell in love with you	Please don't say we'll never find a way
Turned my whole world upside down.	And tell me all my love's in vain.

let it grow

Words & Music by Eric Clapton

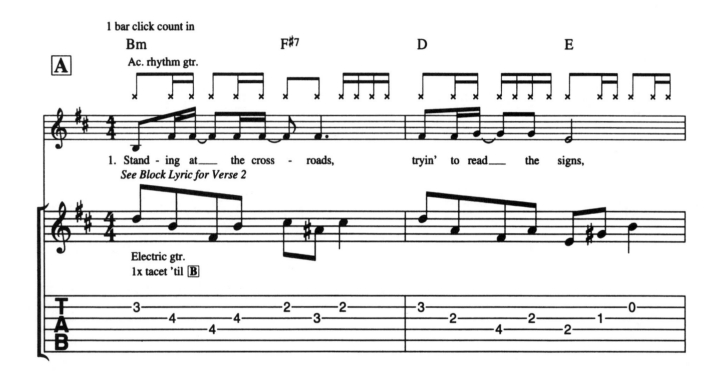

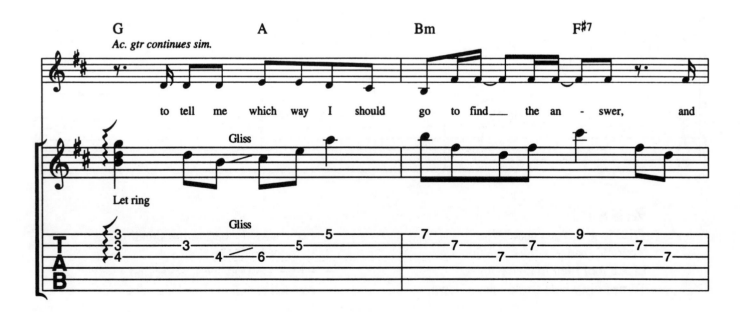

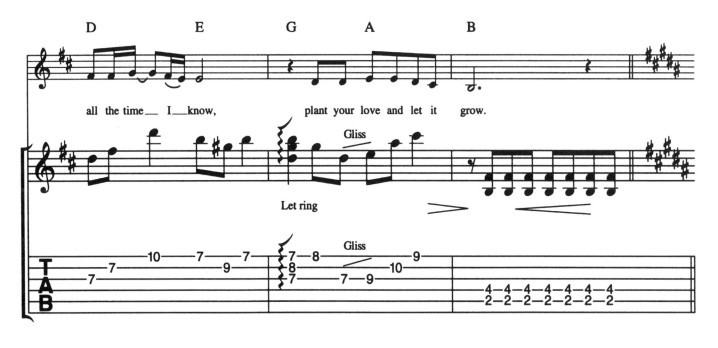

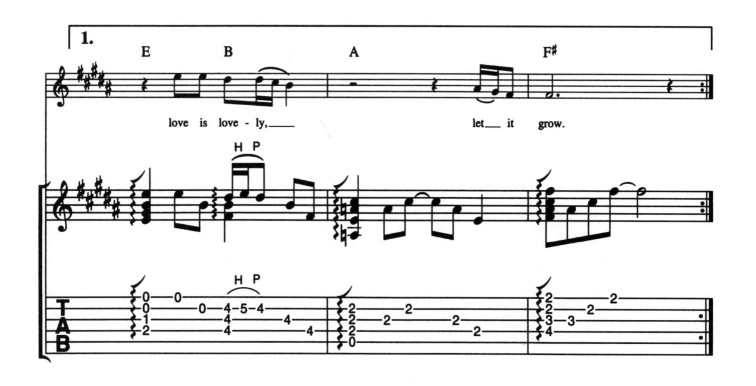

love is love - ly,＿　　　　　　let＿ it　grow.

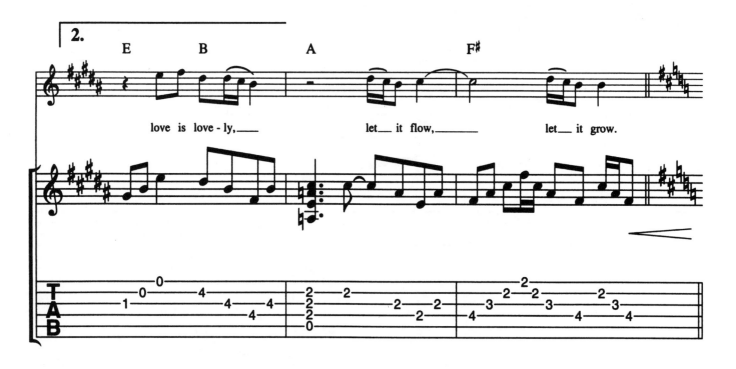

love is love - ly,＿　　　let＿ it flow,＿＿＿　　let＿ it grow.

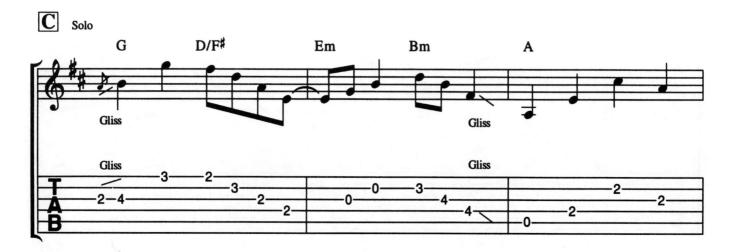

C　Solo

Gliss

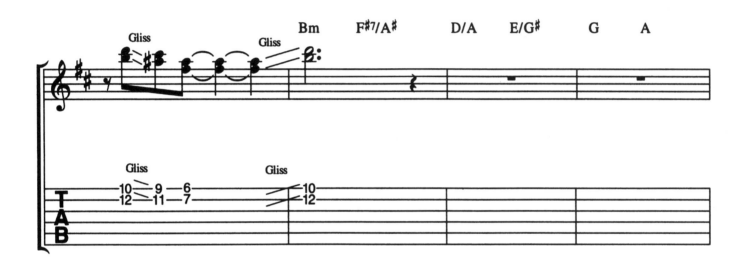

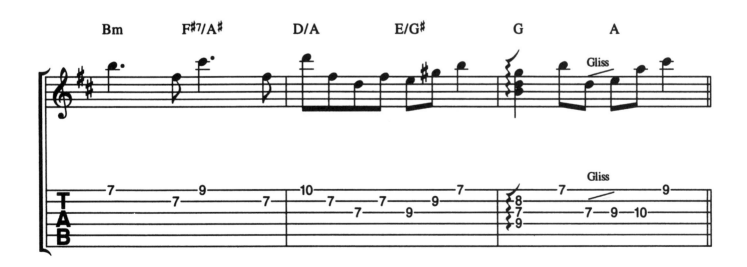

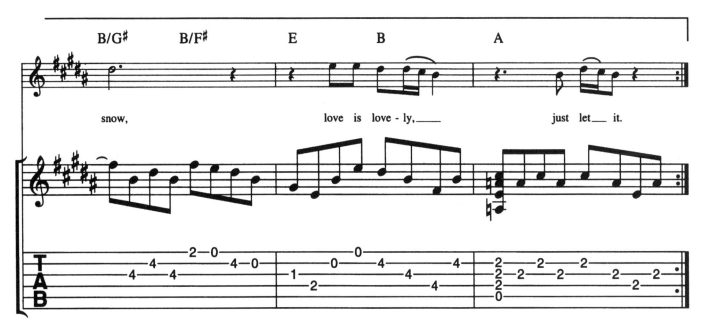

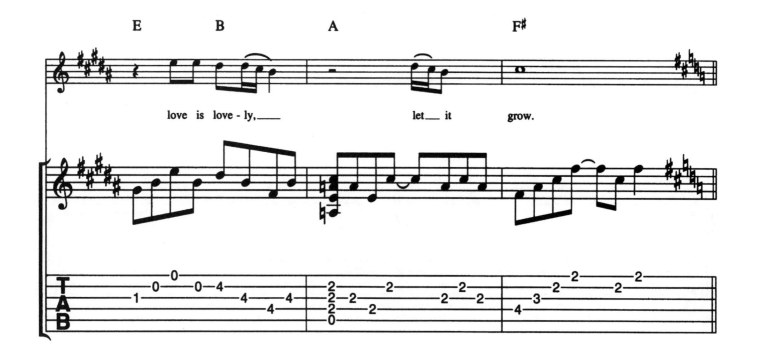

love is love-ly,_____ let_ it grow.

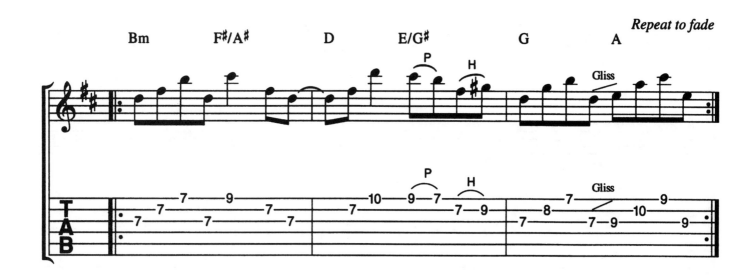

Repeat to fade

Verse 2:
Looking for a reason
To check out in my mind
Find it hard to get a friend
That I can count on
There's nothing left to say
Plant your love and let it grow.

sunshine of your love

Words & Music by Jack Bruce, Pete Brown & Eric Clapton

1 bar click count in

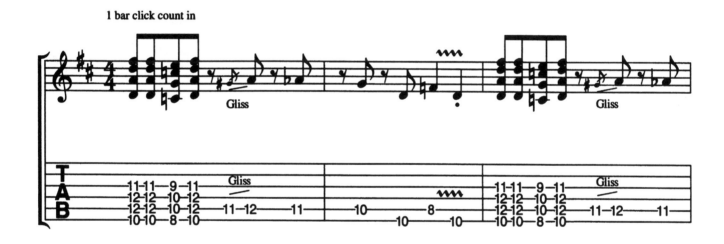

Repeat 3x

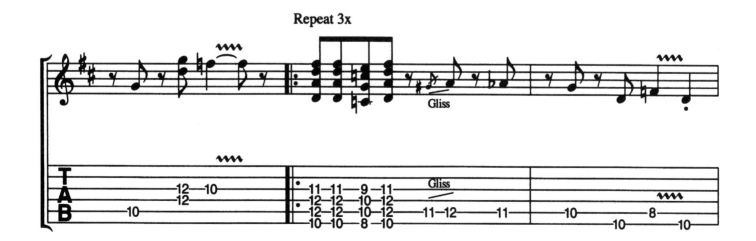

1. Well it's get - ting near dawn,_____ when

See Block Lyrics for Verses 2&3

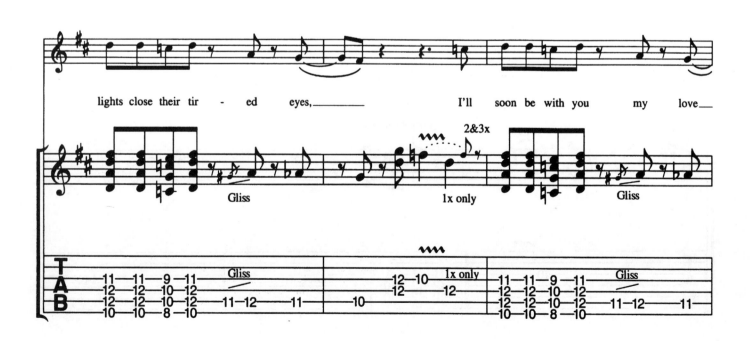

lights close their tir - ed eyes,_____ I'll soon be with you my love_____

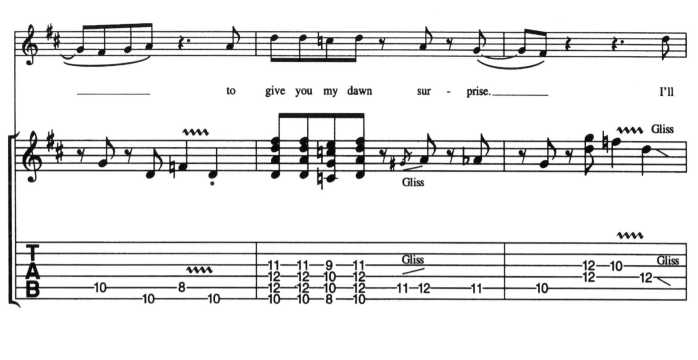

to give you my dawn sur - prise._____ I'll

be with you dar - ling soon,_____ I'll be with you when the stars_____

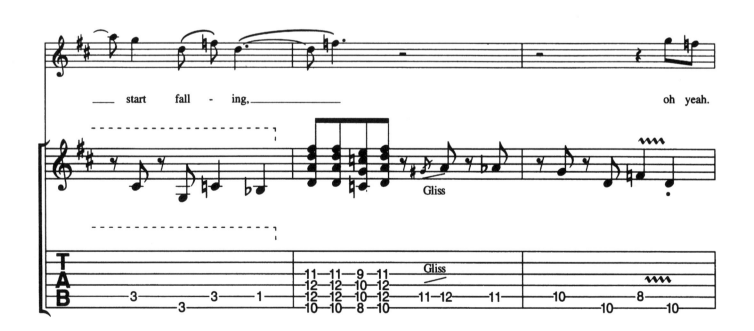

____ start fall - ing,_____ oh yeah.

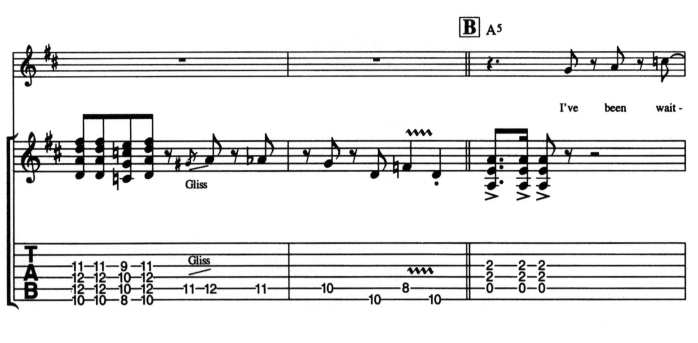

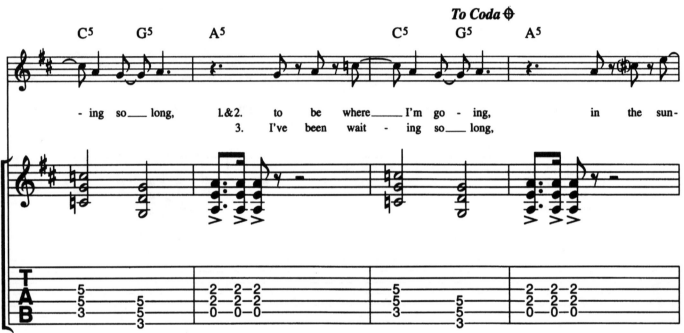

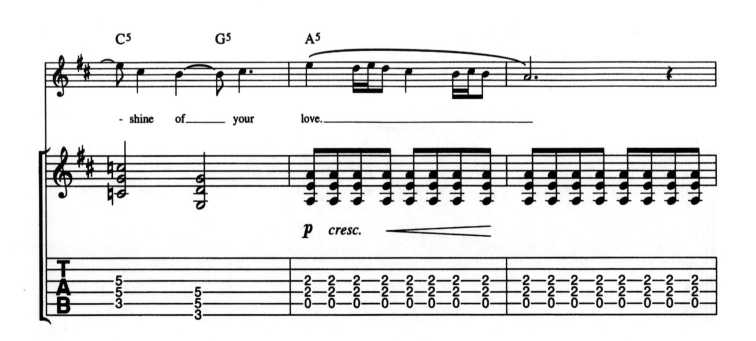

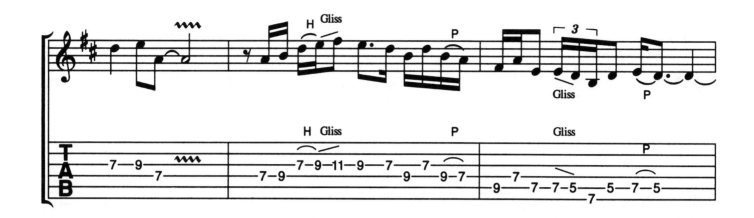

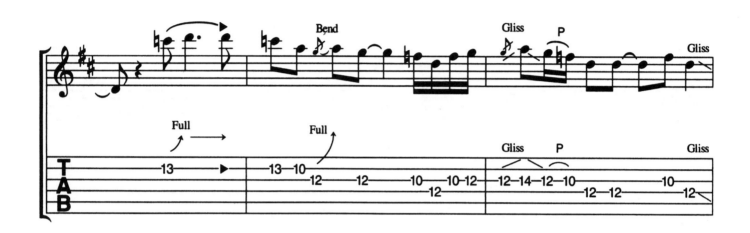

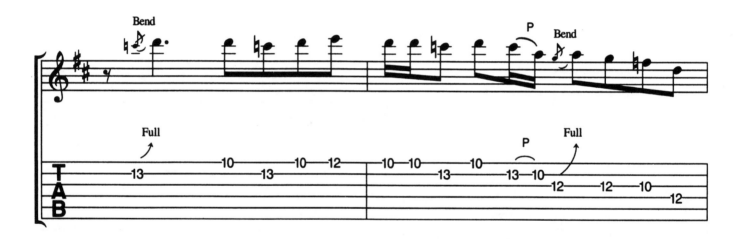

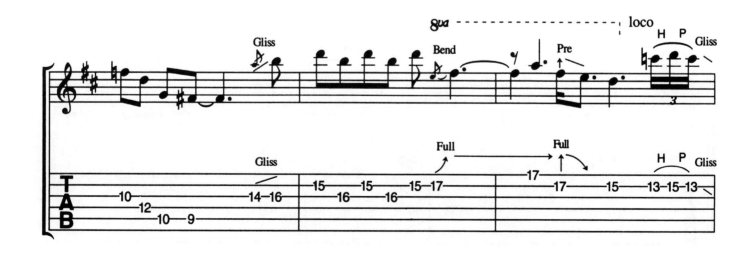

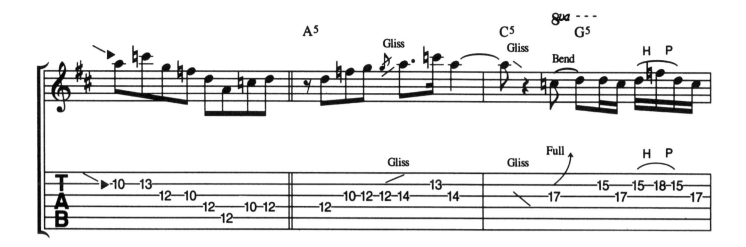

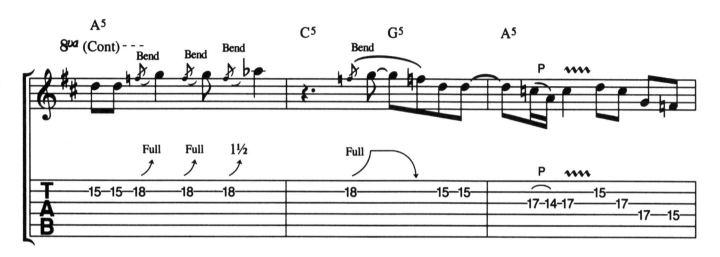

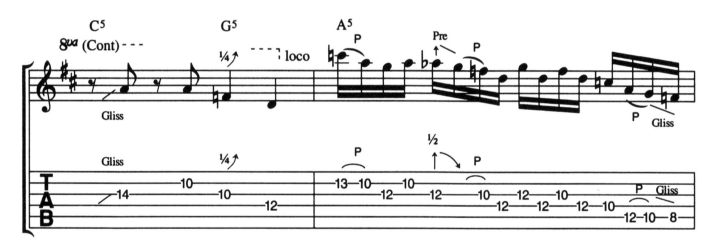

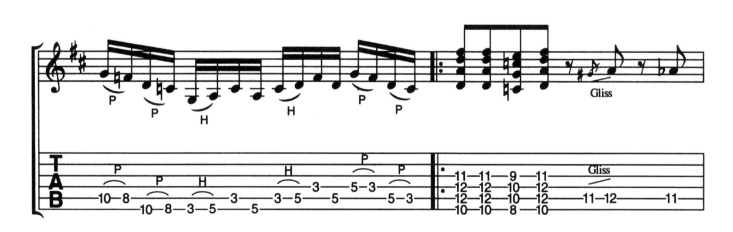

⊕ Coda

to be where_____ I'm go - ing, in the sun - shine of your

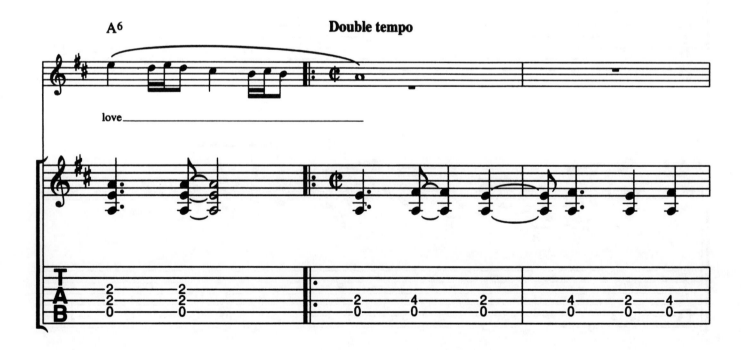

love_____

Double tempo

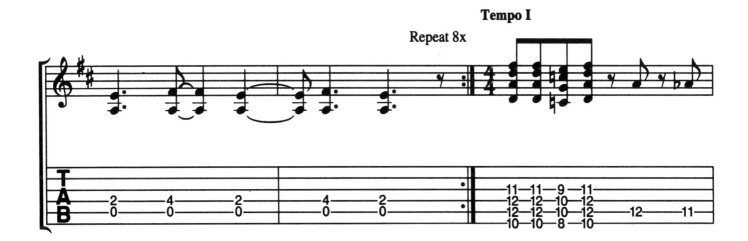

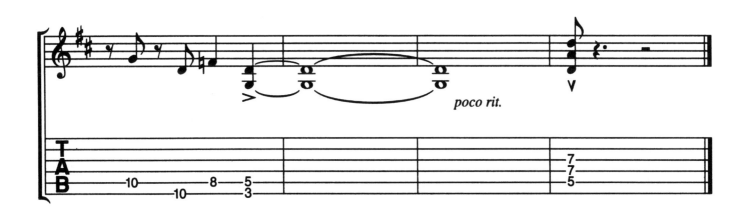

Verse 2:
I'm with you my love
The light's shining through on you
Yes, I'm with you my love.
It's the morning, and just we two.
I'll stay with you darling now
I'll stay with you till my seeds are dried up
(Oh yeah).

Verse 3:
It's getting near dawn
(When) lights close their tired eyes.
I'll soon be with you my love
(To) give you my dawn surprise.
I'll be with you darling soon
I'll be with you when the stars start falling
(Oh yeah).

tears in heaven

Words & Music by Eric Clapton & Will Jennings

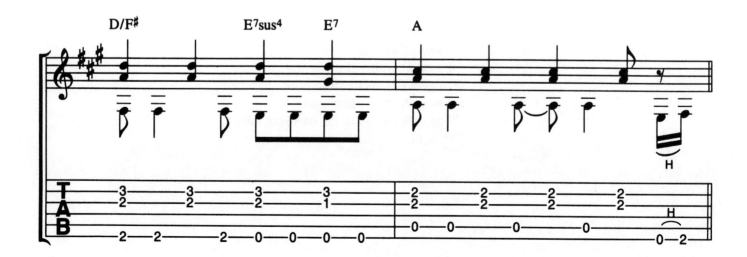

time can bend your knees. ___

Time can break your heart, ___ have ya beg - gin' please, ___ beg - gin' please. ___

2nd gtr solo

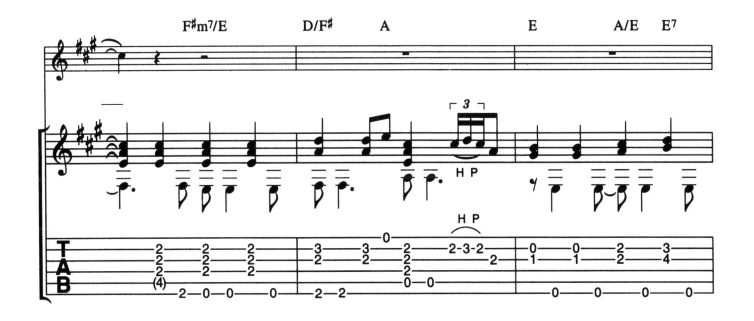

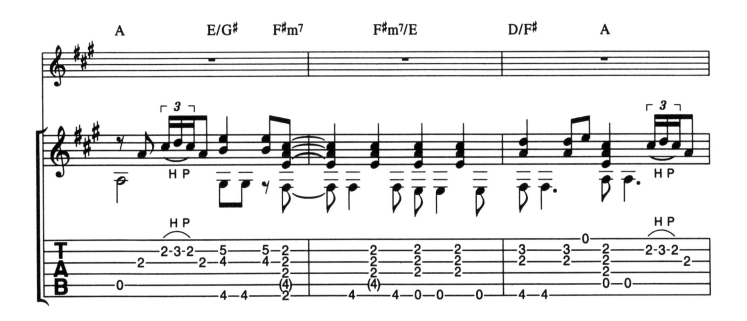

Chorus:

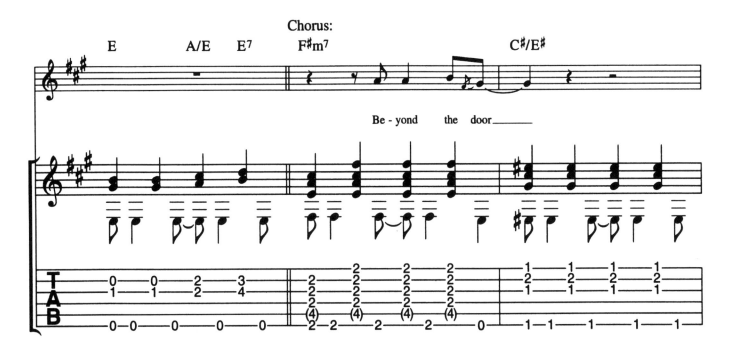

Be - yond   the   door_____

there's peace, I'm sure,_____ and I know there'll be no more_____ tears_____ in hea - ven.

D.%. al $\oplus$ Coda
No repeat

42

⊕ *Coda*

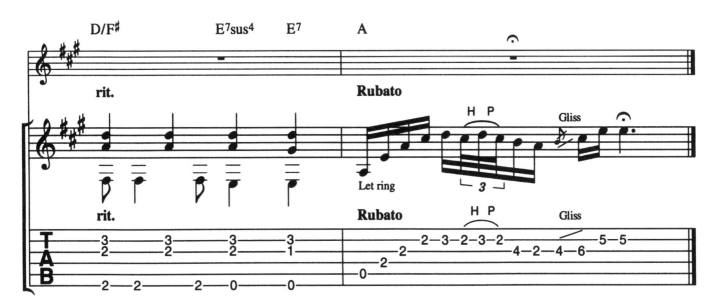

Verse 2:
Would you hold my hand
If I saw you in heaven?
Would you help me stand
If I saw you in heaven?

Chorus 2:
I'll find my way
Through night and day,
'Cause I know I just can't stay
Here in heaven.

Verse 3 (%):
Would you know my name
If I saw you in heaven?
Would you do the same
If I saw you in heaven?

Chorus 3 (%):
I must be strong
And carry on,
'Cause I know I don't belong
Here in heaven.

wonderful tonight

Words & Music by Eric Clapton

1 bar click count in

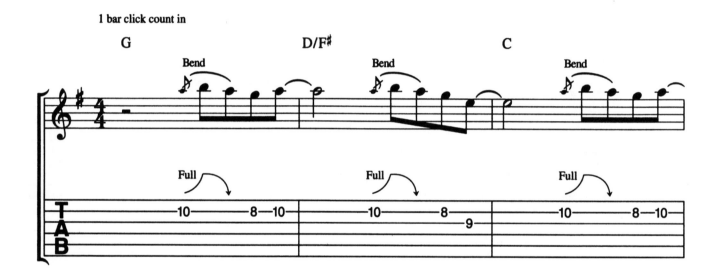

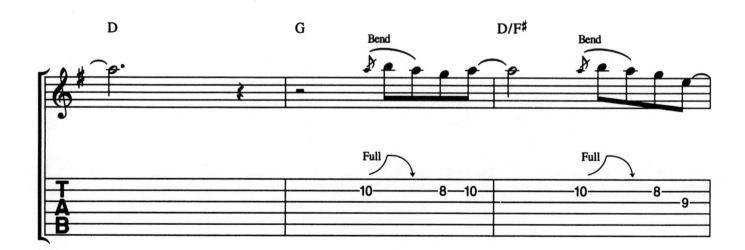

I feel won - der - ful___ be - cause I see___ the love -

- light in___ your eyes.___ Then the won - der of it all___

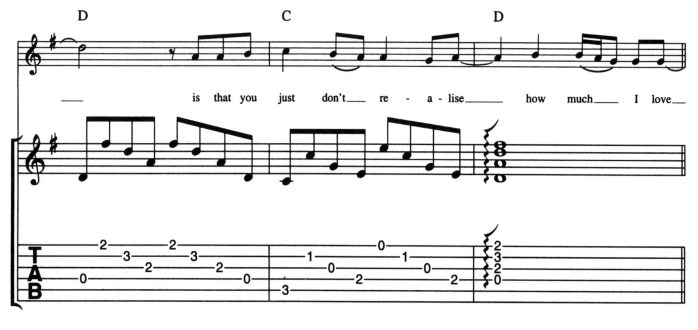

is that you just don't ___ re - a - lise ___ how much ___ I love ___

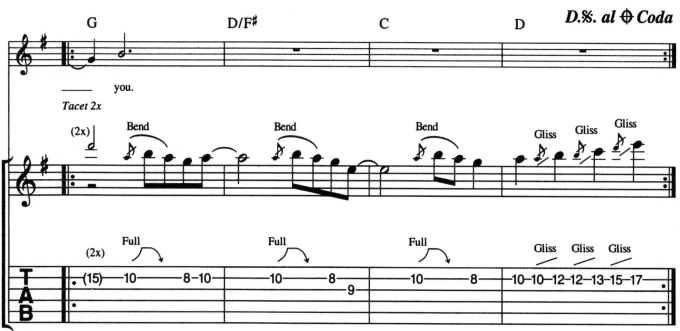

___ you.

Tacet 2x

D.%. al ⊕ Coda

⊕ Coda

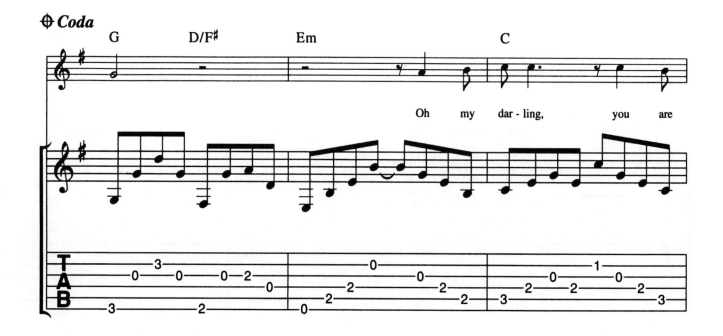

Oh my dar - ling, you are

Verse 2:
We go to a party
And everyone turns to see
This beautiful lady
Is walking around with me
And then she asks me
"Do you feel alright?"
And I say, "Yes,
You look wonderful tonight."

Verse 3:
It's time to go home now
And I've got an aching head
So I give her the car keys
And she helps me to bed
And then I tell her
As I turn out the light
I say, "My darling,
You are wonderful tonight.
Oh my darling,
You are wonderful tonight."

white room

Words & Music by Jack Bruce & Pete Brown

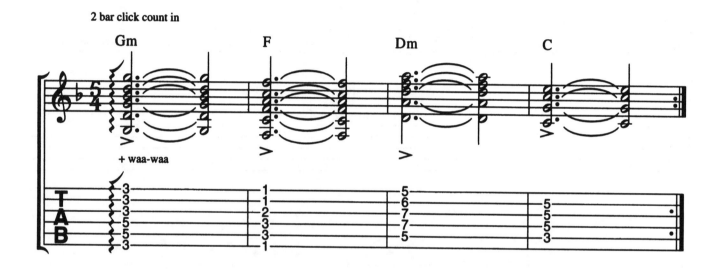

1. In___ a white room___ with black cur - tains, by the sta -

See Block Lyrics for Verses 2&3

52

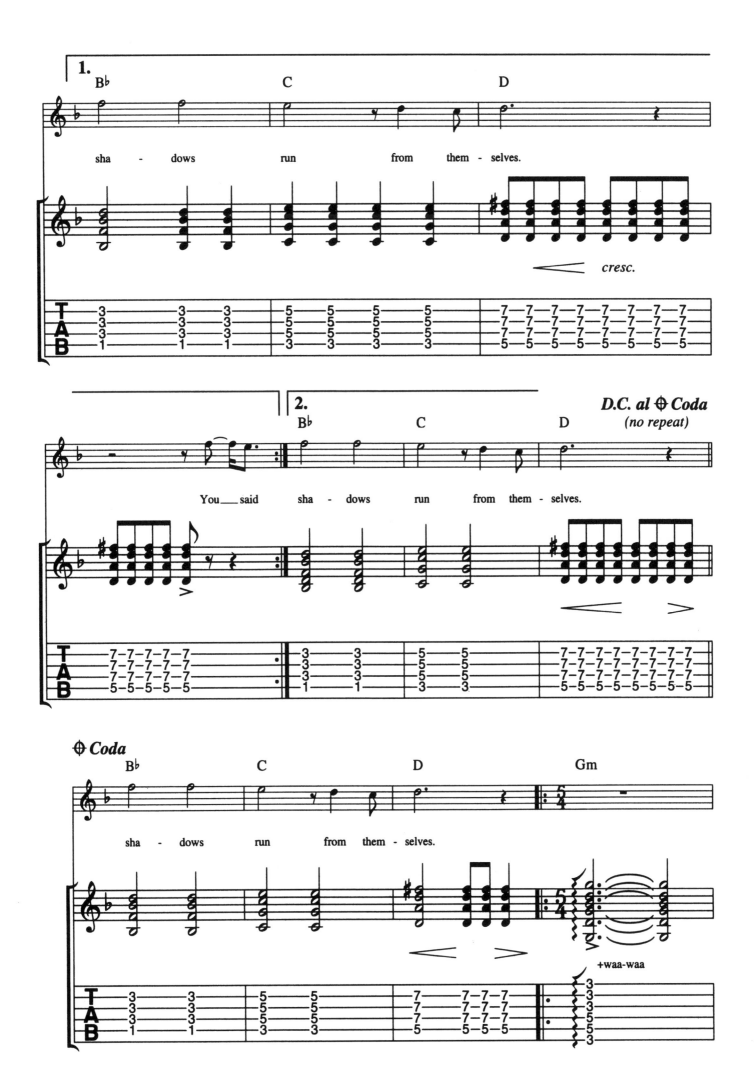

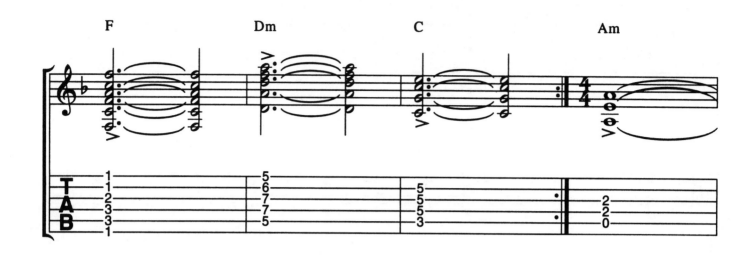

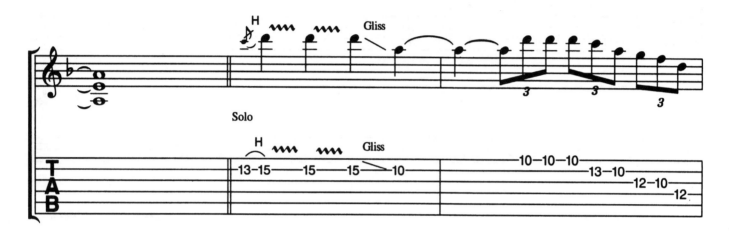

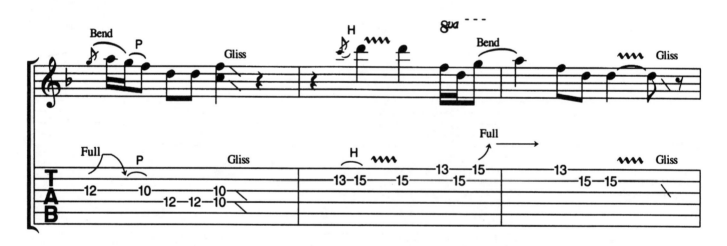

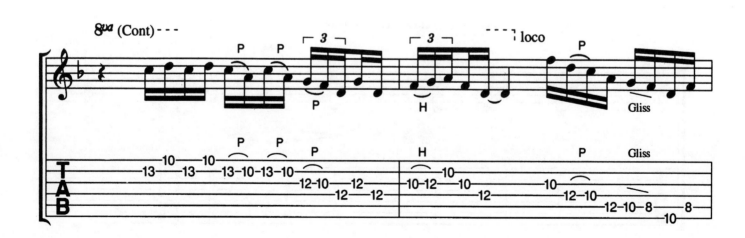

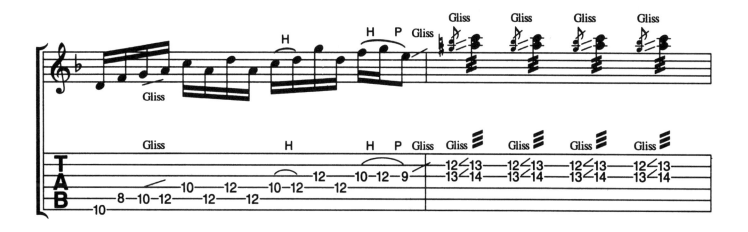

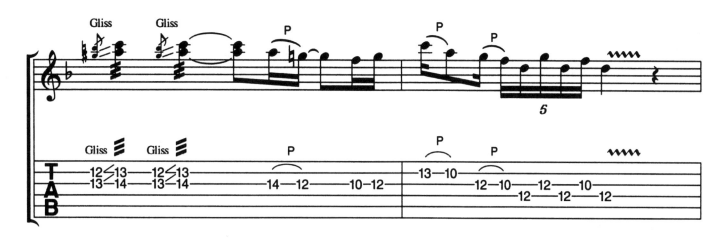

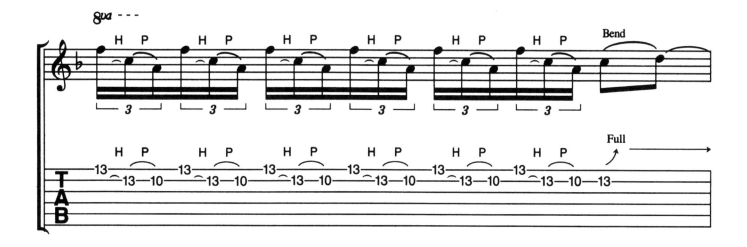

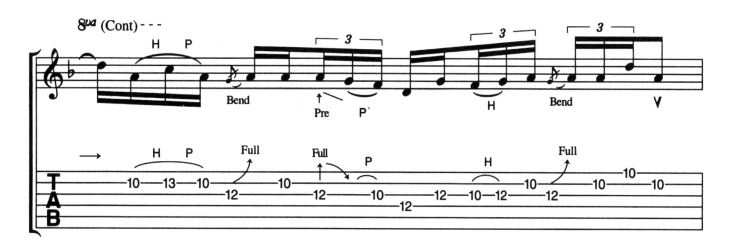

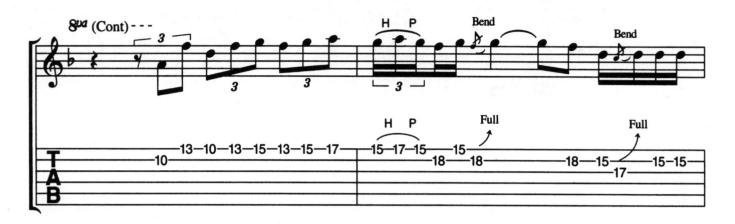

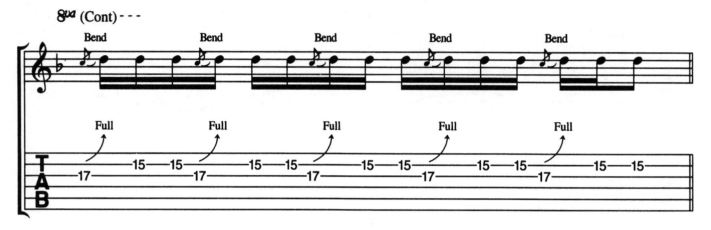

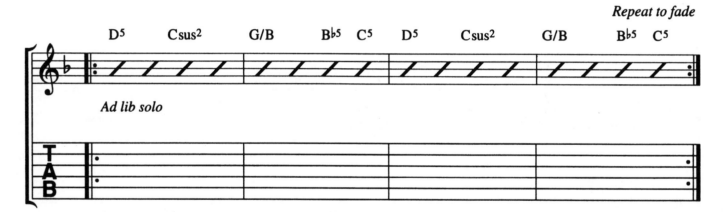

Verse 2:
You said no strings
Could secure you at the station.
Platform ticket, restless diesels,
Goodbye windows,
And I walked into such a sad time
At the station
When I walked out,
Felt my own need
Just beginning.

Chorus 2:
I'll wait in the queue
When the train's gone by
Lie here with you
Where the shadows
Run from themselves.

Verse 3:
At the party she was kindness
In the hard crowd
Consolation from the old wound
Now forgotten.
Yellow tigers crouched in jungles
In the dark eyes
Now she's dressing
Goodbye windows
Tired starlings.

Chorus 3:
I'll wait in this place
Where the sun never shines
Wait in this place
Where the shadows
Run from themselves.

56

9/04 (52558)